Original title:
Swimming in the Abyss

Copyright © 2025 Creative Arts Management OÜ
All rights reserved.

Author: Eleanor Prescott
ISBN HARDBACK: 978-1-80587-393-8
ISBN PAPERBACK: 978-1-80587-863-6

Treacherous Tides

The water's warm but oh so sly,
It pulls your legs, makes you sigh.
You think you're safe, just floating free,
Then suddenly it's trying to swallow thee.

With rubber ducks as my trusty fleet,
I battle waves beneath my feet.
A cannonball makes quite a splash,
While jellyfish slide by with style and panache.

The Deepening Shadow

I dove into a gloomy place,
Where fishes sport a poker face.
They laugh at me, or so I think,
As bubbles rise, I start to sink.

A seaweed crown upon my head,
King of the deep, or so I said.
But all I find is lots of sand,
And tiny crabs that won't shake my hand.

Where the Light Does Not Reach

In the pitch black, I flap and flail,
Like a fish that's lost its tail.
What's that lurking? A shadowed gleam?
Oh wait, just my imagination's scheme!

I whirl and twirl, striking a pose,
In front of mermaids who laugh and doze.
They're sipping tea from seaweed cups,
While I'm caught in my own hiccup hiccups!

Shadows Beneath the Waves

Beneath the waves, the shadows play,
Grinning fish on a dinner tray.
They nibble bits of my old shoe,
And toss a party without a clue.

I try to join, with fins askew,
But every dance, they bid adieu.
The sea is wild, a goofy spree,
I wave goodbye, as they all flee!

Waves of Forgotten Whispers

In a pool so deep, I lost my shoe,
The fish are laughing, they've got a view.
I flail and splash, with grace like a seal,
Echoes of bubbles, it's quite the deal.

My floaty's deflated, I'm sinking in style,
With a snorkel and mask, I grin all the while.
Those mermaid tales, they make me feel grand,
But I'm just a clown, splashing in the sand.

The Weight of Infinite Waters

I jumped with a cannonball, made quite a scene,
My belly flop echoes, what does that mean?
The water is heavy, my antics quite light,
As I sip from the pool, it's a comical sight.

The turtles are judging, they wear tiny frowns,
While I sport my goggles like golden crowns.
Each stroke is a challenge, I'm moving so slow,
But who needs to win? I'm just here for the show.

A Descent into Quietude

I plunged into silence, a dive full of grace,
Wobbled and giggled, I'm losing the race.
Giant rubber ducks, they float in a line,
I wave at the catfish, their smiles divine.

Beneath the surface, a snail gave me sass,
'You call this a swim? Oh, please, come and pass!'
While I bluster and sputter, feeling quite bold,
The secret? My floaty is starting to fold.

Currents of the Unknown

The whirlpool's a merry-go-round of delight,
I spun like a top, what a whimsical sight!
Fish flipped and flopped, joining in my dance,
The octopus winked, he gave me a chance.

With every big splash, my troubles grew small,
As seaweed tickles, I giggle and haul.
The depths are a party, what joy do I find,
In currents of laughter, I leave worries behind.

Echoes of the Past

Frogs with goggles dive so deep,
Only to wake the fish from sleep.
With bubbles blown and laughter loud,
They dance like jesters, quite unbowed.

A whale in socks takes a grand bow,
While squids in hats exclaim, "Wow!"
The octopus plays peek-a-boo,
As sea turtles join in the crew.

Currents of Memory

The seahorse rides a jet ski fast,
While coral clowns perform a cast.
A crab in shades struts down the line,
Snapping photos, feeling fine.

Starfish with saxophones in hand,
Play tunes that make the jelly dance.
In this underwater film, we're stars,
Living the dream beneath the bars.

Glimmering in the Gloom

In murky waters, giggles ring,
As fish parade in diamond bling.
A manta ray does a silly twist,
While eels connect with a flash of mist.

The glow of plankton's neon light,
Turns shadows into pure delight.
With wise old turtles cracking jokes,
The sea's alive with playful folks.

The Depths of Reflection

A pufferfish in shades of blue,
Tries to play peek-a-boo with you.
With laughter echoing in the tides,
The crabby crew just laughs and bides.

A mermaid with a ukulele,
Crafts tunes that are bright and smelly.
Echoes of giggles all around,
In the depths, joy is truly found.

Waves of Solitude

In the pool of my own dread,
I do a cannonball instead.
The water laughs with every splash,
As I wiggle, flop, and crash.

Friends invite me to join their race,
I just float without a trace.
With rubber ducks as my best mates,
We hold the world and laugh at fate.

Navigating the Unseen

Floating on my trusty raft,
I steer through dreams and whimsy craft.
With fish who giggle, oh so sweet,
They swim in circles, so upbeat.

A jellyfish just gave me a wink,
What do they know? I pause to think.
A sea of laughs, a wave of cheers,
I'm lost—but who cares? I'll steer for years!

The Chasm Awaits

Into the unknown, I shall dive,
With a smile that's oh-so-alive.
My fins are tiny, but my heart is grand,
I twirl and swirl, it's all unplanned.

The shadows dance like old-time mimes,
I giggle at their silly climbs.
Just wait till they see my best flip,
Watch out, world, it's a bouncy trip!

Fearful Depths

Below the surface, shadows creep,
But hey, that's where I take my leap!
With rubber fins and a snorkel bright,
I dive headfirst into the night.

A mermaid says, "Ouch! Watch your toes!"
I chuckle as the current flows.
With every splash, I find my muse,
Fearful depths? I choose to cruise!

The Silent Veil of Fog

In the thick of the fog, I waddle and glide,
A sea of confusion, nowhere to hide.
I splashed at a fish, it gave me a wink,
I swear it just chuckled, what do you think?

With each little kick, I spin round and round,
Trying to dodge what I've almost found.
A whirlpool of giggles, or maybe it's me,
Who said deep waters can't spark glee?

An octopus waved, I thought it a friend,
Until it threw ink, my laughter would mend.
I can't tell you why, but I swam through the haze,
In a sea full of jokes, for all of my days.

So here in this swamp of fizz and of fun,
I dance with the bubbles, I'm never done.
If you hear me from shore, don't call out my name,
For me and the fog, we're both quite the same.

A Journey through the Liquid Dark

Down in the deep, where the shadows prowl,
I call out to ghouls, but they all just scowl.
A mermaid popped in, her hair full of slime,
She promised me treasure, just a matter of time.

With my trusty floaty, I bravely descended,
Seeking the laughter, wherever it blended.
Fish told me tales of old sunken ships,
While I just kept bobbing and doing my flips.

But what's that I see in the gloom far ahead?
A laughing sea monster? Perhaps it's misled!
With bubbles for giggles and fins made of joy,
We danced through the waves, oh what a ploy!

And as I surfaced, I couldn't believe,
I had found what I lost, a reason to weave.
In depths full of nonsense, where silliness sways,
A journey so wild, it brightens my days.

Sinking Slowly

I pondered life in the deep blue,
Where fish wear hats and play peek-a-boo.
My goggles fogged, I'd lost my way,
As jellyfish danced, I thought to stay.

A squirrel in a scuba gear,
He waved and grinned, oh what a cheer!
My toes got tickled by seaweed's hand,
I giggled softly, what a strange land!

Unraveled in the Deep

The octopus asked for a game of cards,
While sea turtles rolled in their own yards.
I tried to dive, but tripped on a shell,
And fell on a clam who wished me well.

A whale with shades sang a tune so nice,
As fishes joined in, oh what a device!
I tumbled around in laughter's grip,
With bubbles and giggles, I lost my grip.

Treasures of the Abyss

I found a fork and a shiny old spoon,
A treasure map marked with a cartoon.
Crabs were the guards, they snapped their claws,
While mermaids giggled with gleeful applause.

An anchor grinned, with a rusty smile,
Claiming my loot took quite a while.
But who needs gold when you've got a laugh,
And a pirate fish taking a bubble bath!

A Realm Beyond Sight

Down in the dark where shadows play,
A dancing shrimp led the way.
I lost my flippers and started to swirl,
In a whirlpool of laughter, I gave a twirl.

A toothy grin from a snail in a hat,
Bubbled up jokes, oh imagine that!
In a world so bizarre where silliness reigns,
I splashed through giggles, embracing the gains.

A Descent into Stillness

Diving down, I find that spot,
Where fish wear hats, and time forgot.
A mermaid lass is sipping tea,
While kraken plays the ukulele for me.

The bubbles dance, they pop and swirl,
As I meet a turtle in a twirl.
He winks at me, says, "What's the fuss?"
We giggle at a whale on a bus.

In this quiet place, where silence sings,
I tickle an octopus with bright blue rings.
He throws his arms up, starts to laugh,
It's a comedy show on my underwater path.

So I float around, not much to dread,
In this wacky realm, I just want to tread.
I'll stay here 'til I lose my mind,
This kooky world is hard to find!

Currents of the Unknowable

Waves of jelly, dancing around,
They throw a party, and I've found,
A school of fish in tuxedos bright,
Doing the cha-cha with sheer delight.

There's quite a commotion, a dolphin parade,
With confetti of seaweed, they're unafraid.
A blowfish is popping, who knew he could?
Saying, "Pop my bubbles, it's all understood!"

The water tickles, it all feels grand,
As starfish cheers from the sandy land.
Lost in the current, I follow along,
Singing fishy tunes, where we all belong.

Every twist hides a joke in disguise,
Underwater laughter makes me realize,
That in this deep place, worries just melt,
Even the squid has an air of belt!

Veil of the Depths

Under the waves, a riddle awaits,
With fishy friends and curious mates.
A clam plays chess with a cormorant,
Each checkmate brings on a silly chant.

A pufferfish sporting a polka-dot tee,
Is giving a seminar on how to be free.
While eels tell stories that twist and bend,
Witty little tales that never quite end.

The seaweed sways like a playful dance,
In bubbles, I giggle, caught in a trance.
A crab walks by with a monocle on,
His wise expression says, "Come on, come on!"

Each nook a secret, each corner a jest,
In this underwater realm, I feel so blessed.
No worries to ponder, just laughter ahead,
In the veil of the depths, I'm happily led.

Eldritch Waters

In waters that swirl with shadows so deep,
I found a sea witch who couldn't stop to sleep.
Her cauldron bubbles with odd-shaped snacks,
She serves me kelp chips with gacky cracks.

A ghostly fish flits by with a wink,
He says, "Stand back! Or I'll make you stink!"
With pearly scales, it swirls like a kite,
It's the funniest sight in the dead of night.

With tentacles waving, a sea monster shouts,
'Why don't you join me? I'm full of doubts!'
We do a quick jig, though he's quite enormous,
Got me questioning if I'm truly a former-us.

Each creature has quirks, and jokes to tell,
In these eldritch waters, all's quite swell.
So let's wade deeper into the unknown,
Where laughter prevails, and joy is our own!

Echoes Beneath the Waves

Bubbles rise up, tickling toes,
I lost my goggles, now I doze.
Fish parade in silly hats,
Swimming past the silly spats.

The octopus laughs, paints my face,
I wave back in this goofy place.
Mermaids giggle, they're in on the joke,
Here I float, a laughing bloke.

Seaweed wraps me like a hug,
Tangled up, oh what a snug!
The crab starts a conga line,
Who knew that depths could be so fine?

Echoes bounce off coral walls,
As dolphins share their comedy calls.
In this blue and funny dance,
I take a plunge, and bid my prance.

Beneath the Glassy Calm

The surface gleams, so oddly lied,
I belly flop, then I slide.
A walrus winks, and takes a dive,
In this calm, I feel so alive.

The starfish tries to play the fool,
While I'm here, bending the rule.
Jellyfish float like flying kites,
In this tranquil world, we share delights.

The sea turtle with a top hat,
Waves hello, oh, fancy that!
Anemones dance with flair,
Underneath this calm affair.

Fish are gossiping all day,
About the swimmers, come what may.
I'm just here for laughs and splashes,
In this glassy calm, joy never crashes.

In the Grip of the Abyss

In the grip of something deep,
I find myself in a jelly heap.
A shrimp applauds my stealthy glide,
As I twirl and bump, oh what a ride!

Down here, the fish play hide and seek,
Chasing bubbles, squeaks and squeaks.
Clams giggle behind their shells,
Telling tales of underwater smells.

A grouper's got a knock-knock knack,
While I'm lost in this wobbly track.
I think I saw a dancing rock,
But it was just a spooked-out sock.

The depths are a carnival of glee,
With krakens cracking jokes at me.
In this grip, I dance and sway,
Under waves of laughter, come what may.

The Weight of Stillness

In the stillness, it's quite a feat,
I'm stuck to the floor, can't move my feet.
A stingray glides, I'm just a rock,
Spelling 'help' in seaweed shock.

But the clownfish come with a show,
Swirling and twirling, putting on a glow.
I can't resist, I join in the fun,
Who knew being still could weigh a ton?

An urchin grins, spins its spikes,
As I float around, sharing my likes.
A sea cucumber joins the parade,
In this stillness, a joy cascade.

So here I am, a buoyant ball,
With fishy friends, oh how they enthrall.
In the weight of stillness, laughter sings,
I'm anchored in joy, still pulling strings.

Dark Currents

In the depths where shadows play,
Fishes swim the wrong way.
They giggle as they twist and twine,
Bumping heads, oh what a line!

Eels throw parties, slipping fast,
While crabs read stories of the past.
Jellyfish dance, glowing and bright,
Who knew the dark could bring such light?

Mermaids sing off-key with glee,
Critters joining, a wild spree.
Caught in laughter, they all forget,
That soon they might be someone's pet!

So if you wander where the sun fades,
Join the fun in aquatic parades.
Just remember, take care in the slide,
One misstep, and you're seafood fried!

Descent into Night

Falling fast through velvet gloom,
I arrived at a bizarre room.
Octopuses knitted sweaters wide,
While turtles posed with bottom pride!

"Do the crab," the conch did shout,
As bubbles formed and danced about.
I tried, but tripped upon a whale,
Who laughed so hard, it shook the sail!

Bubbles tickled my funny bone,
As starfish told jokes of their own.
With every flip, I lost my way,
But who cared? We were here to play!

With glowing smiles, we rolled along,
In the dark, where all belong.
And though I strolled through depths unknown,
I found a home — I shouldn't have flown!

Beneath the Still Surface

Just below where the stillness rests,
Silly fish put on comedy tests.
Tadpoles tap danced near by,
While pond frogs croaked a lullaby.

Suddenly, a rock went thud,
A massive splash — it was the stud!
"Who dropped me?" he called, all aghast,
But laughter echoed; it was a blast!

We played pelota with a seaweed ball,
As snails joined in the laughter's thrall.
The water swirled with giggles galore,
A bubbling sea of jokes to explore!

So if you want a good laugh today,
Dive below for the joyful fray.
Beneath the calm, there's a raucous cheer,
With creatures who'll tickle your funny sphere!

The Forgotten Depths

In a realm where the foolish swim,
Creatures play a prank on a whim.
Lost keys to treasure, laugh and shout,
"Who took our stuff?" then they pout!

With goggle-eyed fish making big fuss,
A clam threw a party on the bus.
The guest list featured squid and flounder,
While snappy turtles went in rounds, sir!

"What's the deal with seaweed wraps?"
But the lobsters just fell into traps.
They danced too hard, forgot the beat,
And suddenly all got cold feet!

Though depths are forgotten, we're far from sad,
In silly chaos, we've always had.
So come on down and join the fun,
In these waters, you'll never run!

Submerged in Elysium's Grief

I dove into the depths with glee,
But found a crab that spoke to me.
It asked for change, a dollar bill,
To buy a snack—what a thrill!

The fish all laughed at my surprise,
With bubble wands and sparkling eyes.
They danced in swimsuits, tails a-flare,
While I just floundered, gasping air.

A mermaid giggled, hands on hips,
Offered me some seaweed chips.
I tried one mouthful, what a taste!
And then I flew—oh, what a waste!

So here I float, my days of bliss,
Amongst the kelp; what did I miss?
Elysium's sighs, a sea of jest,
Where even sharks can take a rest!

The Abyssal Reverie

With fins like fluttering flag parade,
I dreamt of a fish grand escapade.
But jellybeans were all I found,
In gooey depths, oh what a clown!

An octopus wore a fancy hat,
And spun me tales of jazz and chat.
We danced on currents, smooth and sleek,
Where silence laughs, but none can speak.

Eels were lining up for a show,
Reciting poems, deep and low.
I cheered them on, though lost my breath,
In rhyming songs of silly death.

At last, I found a treasure chest,
Filled with snacks and a squishy vest.
Who knew the deep could hold such cheer?
I'll stay down here, let's disappear!

Fantasia of the Depths

In the deep where giggles flowed,
A chorus of turtles formed a road.
They taught me how to play the lute,
While sea cucumbers danced in a suit.

I wore a crown of coral bling,
Declared myself the seaweed king.
But little fish called me a fool,
For wearing green in a fishy pool!

Jellyfish pranced in rainbow hues,
With dancing lights, oh how they cruise!
I tried to join the disco throng,
But tripped on waves; it felt so wrong.

Yet laughter bubbled, all around,
In this place where joy abound.
So here's to fun beneath the wave,
Where even sea stars misbehave!

Navigating the Obsidian Sea

In waters dark, I lost my map,
A penguin offered me a nap.
Together we drifted, quite a sight,
Playing catch with a gleaming light.

A narwhal hummed a catchy tune,
While squids joined in, beneath the moon.
We formed a band, oh what a dream,
In twilight's veil, we learned to beam.

The krakens tried to join our fun,
But tangled in a net—a run!
They plopped about, oh what a mess,
While I just laughed, in joyous stress.

So as I float on waves of cheer,
In this obsidian sea so dear,
I'll weave my tales, I'll bend the light,
And dance with friends through day and night!

Treading Water in Darkness

In murky depths, I take a dip,
Where even fish have lost their grip.
I paddle with a flailing grace,
Hoping to find a friendly face.

Goggles on, I'm quite the sight,
Splashing 'round in the dead of night.
With every wave, I laugh and flail,
A comedy act in this dark tale.

I thought I'd be a graceful swan,
But more like a duck that's overdrawn.
Fish rolling eyes, they swim on by,
As I bubble up a silly sigh.

The Abyssal Dance

In the depths where no one can see,
I twirl and spin, just like a bee.
With an ocean floor as my dance floor,
I shimmy and shake, want to dance more!

My fins are flapping, I'm in a trance,
Creating ripples, it's quite the chance.
Crabs pinch my toes, they join the fun,
Underwater rave, oh what a run!

With a jellyfish doing the wave,
And seaweed tangled, I must behave.
But what's a dance without some flair?
I moonwalk sideways without a care.

Currents of Despair

Caught in a tide that pulls me down,
I wave hello to a much-frowning clown.
He offers me a soggy sandwich,
In this deep place where nothing can banish.

With every gulp, I feel less bright,
As I paddle through this murky plight.
The more I struggle, the less I thrive,
My fishy friends say, 'Just stay alive!'

Why's everyone frowning? What's their deal?
I try a cartwheel, they don't appeal.
Fins talking smack, oh what a scene,
They have a phobia of my routine!

Beneath the Surface

Bubbles rise like giggly jokes,
As I tumble with the gurgling yokes.
The bottom line is quite a mess,
With sea turtles having a dress.

I peek at fish in trendy shades,
Who scoff at my glubbed charades.
They swim past me with style and grace,
While I'm just lost in this silly place.

But let them stare, I'll play it cool,
With every wave, I make my rule.
This chaos brings a joyful cheer,
In depths so wild, I find my sphere.

Lost in the Vortex

Around I twirl, like a sock in a wash,
I find my left foot with a clammy little squish.
The whirlpool spins, like it's hosting a dance,
My belly does flip-flops, oh what a romance.

Giant fish give me a bewildered stare,
As I bobble along, I float through the air.
"What's that human doing?" they say with a grin,
I'll teach them my moves, oh let the fun begin!

A jellyfish giggles, coast on my head,
We're partners in crime as we drift with the thread.
I slip and I slide, like a squid on a skate,
This underwater circus, oh isn't it great?

At last, I resurface, a sight truly grand,
With seaweed in hand, I strike up a band.
Now fish throw confetti as bubbles come forth,
Lost in this whirlpool, I've found my true worth.

The Ethereal Plunge

Fins on my feet, I'm a mermaid tonight,
Splashing with turtles, oh what a delight!
I dive to the depths with a tickle and giggle,
The octopus joins in, he twirls and he wiggles.

The seaweed tosses, it's a dance hall of green,
Dancing with crabs, who are awfully mean!
They pinch my poor toes, give a comical squeeze,
I dance away quickly, move like a breeze.

A shark named Barry sings karaoke so loud,
His pitch is a miracle, he draws quite a crowd.
I join for a duet, our voices collide,
An anthem of bubbles that bounces with pride.

As the currents rock gently, I float with a yawn,
A whale joins the chorus, all the worries are gone.
In this tide of laughter, I find pure bliss,
With jokes from the depths, how could I resist?

Abyssal Whispers

Down in the gloom where the big fish zoom,
I hear a voice calling, 'It's time for some room!'
With a chuckle and flip, I bump into a seal,
He juggles some shells while spinning a wheel.

Crustaceans gossip of secrets so sly,
'Why did the clam cross the ocean?' 'To fry!'
I chuckle and snort as I dive through the tease,
In this realm of humor, it's filled with the bees.

A manta ray glides, with a wink and a flip,
His joke about sea cucumbers makes me trip.
Giggles echo softly through bubbles and foam,
In this comical world, I've truly found home.

As I glide through the trenches, mischief in store,
Crab sends a wink—there's always room for more.
With each little whisper, I laugh and I spin,
What's a little abyss when the fun's about to begin?

Veins of Silence

In the deep where the sunbeams have failed to appear,
I tumble and roll, no worries or fear.
Eels twist and shout in a silent ballet,
Their moves are like whispers, perfect for play.

A ghostly shark glides, he's a master of stealth,
But his clumsy ballet is bad for his health.
As I giggle and dodge, he fumbles and slips,
Chasing his tail—watch those turbulent trips!

The quiet is broken by bubbles that pop,
I'm the jester here, never wanting to stop.
I flip like a dolphin through currents of cheer,
A dance in the silence, where laughter is clear.

So here's to the depths, where fun truly beams,
In the veins of still water, we float on our dreams.
With a wave and a wink, I bid the abyss,
Filled with laughter and joy, a most precious kiss.

The Dark Embrace of Water

Bubbles rise like giggling sprites,
While fish wear tiny party hats.
I've lost my socks to slippery nights,
And there's a crab that's judging my spats.

The deep is like a wiggly joke,
Where seaweed tickles every dive.
My floaties burst, I start to choke,
But laughter helps me stay alive.

The depths play pranks, oh what a spree,
With whirlpools swirling round my feet.
The jellyfish throw a raucous tea,
And I can't find my other sheet.

As shadows dance in playful glee,
The eels are putting on a show.
I'll join them for a wild encore,
But hope I don't get caught, oh no!

Fathoms of Forgotten Souls

Here in the gloom, the fishes grin,
With secrets lost in waters wide.
A dancing fin, a cheeky spin,
And I'm just here along for the ride.

The octopus plays peek-a-boo,
With eight arms waving all about.
I try to copy, but lose my shoe,
And now my feet just want to pout.

Mermaids giggle in shiny scales,
Stirring trouble with bubbly pranks.
With tales of ships and ghostly wails,
They serve seaweed on fine planks.

The wrecks are where the treasures lie,
But I just find a rubber duck.
It's quacking loudly, oh my oh my,
I guess this deep dive's out of luck!

Nurtured by Shadows

In murky waters, I skip and spin,
The sea cucumbers cheer my flair.
Caught in currents but grinning wide,
While seahorses braid my hair.

A clam shouts out, 'Why are you here?'
I shrug, it's just my crazy fate.
This underwater world is dear,
And the laughter's all first-rate.

A treasure chest? Oh wait, just junk!
With mismatched forks and a rusty key.
But here in shadows, it's all fun punk,
As I float like a leaf on a spree.

The bubbles burst with giggles bright,
Dancing around this wavy bay.
In every twist, there's sheer delight,
In this watery game we play!

Whispers from the Deep

The fish gather round for gossip, dear,
  They bubble tales of all their woes.
  I join the blues, forget my fear,
While a friendly stingray strikes a pose.

  With funny hats and wiggly tricks,
  The dolphins toss a beach ball round.
I'm soaked and shriek, a hit from slicks,
Then drift off, laugh-off a splashy sound.

The shipwreck holds a crew of jesters,
  With anchor chains and silly words.
  They tell me life's about the testers,
  Making jokes while sipping on birds.

  Whispers swirl in liquid glee,
While I float by, just one more dive.
  In depth's embrace, I find the key,
To laughter's wave, where all survive!

Voyage into the Void

In the dark where fish wear hats,
A whale's a jester, full of spats.
Mermaids laugh at my sunburned toes,
While octopuses try on my clothes.

I paddled hard through bubble tea,
Dancing with rays that tickle me.
A seahorse kicked just like a pro,
And told me jokes that stole the show.

I grabbed a starfish for a snack,
But it just waved and said, "Step back!"
Anemones play a game of tag,
While sharks just grin with a crazy wag.

So here's to the depths where giggles reign,
Where every splash is a comical gain.
With creatures strange and humor vast,
This voyage is a blast, unsurpassed!

Lurking Beneath

Under the waves, I can't help but sigh,
A crab in a tuxedo passing by.
With bubbles blown and laughter shared,
The depths below are never scared.

Eels in tuxes, ready to impress,
Twirling around like they're at a fest.
A sea cucumber playing the fool,
While jellyfish swim in a dazzling school.

Fish offer snacks from a gourmet spread,
I munch on kelp, feeling quite fed.
An otter dives with a charming quirk,
Snoozing off after all the work.

So if you hear a giggle float by,
It's just me and my pals, oh my!
In this ocean where shenanigans flow,
Lurking beneath, where the funny fish grow.

The Call of the Deep

In the depths where oddities thrive,
A narwhal sings, making vibes come alive.
I answer the call with a splash and a dive,
To join the fun, oh what a jive!

A school of clowns with fins and bright hair,
Telling tales of fish who dare.
They flip and twirl, causing quite a scene,
As seadragons dance in their seaweed green.

A beluga whale cracks a joke so sly,
While penguins waddle, adding to the sky.
Each wave rolls in with a frothy cheer,
Encouraging all to lean in, not fear.

So heed the call of the watery cheer,
In the laughter below, we find what's dear.
Embracing the deep with a chuckle and grin,
In this funny realm, let the joy begin!

Chilling Waters

In chilling waters where the laughter flows,
A fish in shorts throws fantastic throws.
With a splash and a squirt, the fun begins,
Dolphins flip while a clam just grins.

The icebergs wave, "We're chilling too!"
While seals join in for a frosty brew.
Polar bears dance on floating ice,
In a silly, slippery game, so nice!

A crab makes me his funny hat,
While sea lions laugh just like that.
As bubbles rise with giggles and cheer,
These chilling waters bring warmth near.

So take a dip and join the fun,
In this icy realm, there's laughter for everyone.
With every ripple, joy will sprout,
In chilling waters, let's dance about!

The Weight of Water

I jumped into the pool, so bold and spry,
My belly flopped and splashed, oh me, oh my!
I thought I'd glide like a fish on a spree,
But all I did was send waves to the sea.

I swore my goggles were the best around,
Yet they fogged up like a lost circus clown.
With every stroke I took, I'd sink and swerve,
In this wacky aquatic game, I couldn't preserve.

Now I float like a cork, with snacks in tow,
While dolphins giggle, mocking my slow flow.
But I raise my hand for help, in a grand jest,
"Just call me the sea snail; I'm on a quest!"

So I sip my drink, in my noodle chair,
While fish swim past with a condescending stare.
I wave back cheerfully; it's all in good fun,
In this watery world, I'll always be the one.

In the Heart of the Deep

I dove deep down with a cannonball cheer,
Only to find some crabs were sipping beer.
They offered me a shell, said 'Join our feast!'
A party underwater, to say the least.

My fishy friends all danced in a line,
With bubbles rising up like sweet champagne wine.
I twirled and I twisted, having a ball,
But tangling my limbs—oh, that was the fall!

A squid named Larry wanted to show me a trick,
He spun me around; I felt like a brick.
"Enjoy the ride!" he hollered with glee,
As I tumbled past jellyfish, gaping at me.

But laughter erupted from the octopus crew,
As I struggled to swim in a water ballet too.
With a wink and a grin, I joined in the mess,
For the joy of the deep was my ultimate quest.

Churning Waters

The tide rolled in with a boisterous roar,
I thought I'd surf it, oh what a score!
But the moment I stood, the board did a flip,
And I landed face-first with a thunderous dip.

My buddy laughed, said, "You've got no style!
Let me show you how to ride the wave and smile!"
But when he tried to impress, he missed the crest,
And we both got swallowed, what a soggy jest!

We popped back up, drenching wet and loud,
Surrounded by seaweed, we formed a cloud.
"Next time," I said, "let's just build a sand fort,
Where the only tide is our snack-report!"

With pretzels and chips, we'd lounge by the sea,
No more wild adventures that end in a spree.
For nothing beats laughter, henceforth I decree,
In churning waters, it's best to just be free.

An Underworld of Thought

Beneath the surface, thoughts twist and twine,
With sea turtles pondering, "Is this snack divine?"
I swam past a school of fish with a jest,
"Is this an ocean, or a watery fest?"

In reefs filled with colors, I scratched my head,
"Does this coral glow, or did I eat bad bread?"
The angelfish giggled, showing their teeth,
As I twirled through the bubbles, a dance in the sheath.

The starfish blurted, "Hey, let's form a crew!
We'll discuss our duties while sipping on dew!"
But I just floated, not caring at all,
As the whales serenaded, their bass a grand call.

So while they debated the meaning of waves,
I juggled some shells, and I called them my knaves.
For in this deep realm, so funny and bright,
Laughter's the treasure that carries me light.

Depths of Silent Currents

In the deep where the turtles laugh,
And the fish take polite photographs,
I tried a dive, but oh what a show,
Twisted my fins, put on quite a glow.

Bubbles rise, like thoughts in a rush,
I compete with an octopus, oh what a crush,
He juggles shells, I've lost the game,
Swirling around, who's to blame?

The depths here are filled with silly tricks,
Like mermaids playing their jazzy licks,
I float by, a starfish waves me through,
"Dance with the shadows, it's just me and you!"

But just as I'm ready to join the parade,
I trip on a seaweed, how rude, such a charade,
In the depths where I meant to be free,
I find laughter is the best therapy.

Echoes Beneath the Surface

In the waves where the echoes make noise,
I found myself playing with seaweed toys,
A dolphin passed, doing a twist,
While I sank down, thinking, "What did I miss?"

The fish threw a party, bright as a dream,
With coral confetti and a sea cucumber scheme,
I showed off my moves, a flop and a flop,
The ocean erupted, it just wouldn't stop.

I thought I looked smooth, like a whale in the flow,
But a crab called me clumsy, oh me, oh no!
I waved my arms, like I had no control,
"Just practicing moves for my big underwater role!"

With tickling currents and glints in the dark,
I joined the parade, a quirkier shark,
When the bubbles burst, my giggles did swell,
In the vast seas below, all was merry and well.

Drowning in Shadows

In murky waters where giggles convene,
I paddled around like a clumsy machine,
A lobster waved, "Hey, what's the fuss?"
I replied with a splash that made quite the bus.

The flashlight fish glimmer, with antics galore,
They wink and they dance, always wanting more,
I tried to join in, a synchronized flop,
But tripped on my fins, and over I drop.

I find the light beneath a blanket of gloom,
With shadows that shuffle and swirl in their womb,
A seahorse chuckled, saying, "Don't you fret,
Just breathe and let loose, no need for regret!"

I spun with the currents, let laughter bubble,
Even the deep had a sprinkle of trouble,
So I floated along, embracing the night,
In this shadows' embrace, everything felt right.

Embracing the Darkness Below

In the dark where the jellyfish glow,
I giggle and wiggle, just go with the flow,
A squid threw a party, bright and absurd,
But I missed my cue, couldn't get in my word.

With creatures who danced in the soft, eerie light,
I stumbled and tumbled, what a ridiculous sight,
The sea cucumbers laughed with delight,
As I swirled in confusion, lost in my plight.

Octopus chefs served a feast of weird snacks,
I tried to partake but fell flat on my back,
With giggles and bubbles, the laughter rang clear,
I rolled with the tides, nothing left to fear.

So here in the depths, with a grin ear to ear,
I embraced all the madness without any fear,
In this whimsical dark, a treasure I found,
When humor's a current, we all are unbound.

Labyrinth of the Undercurrents

In the depths where goldfish meet,
I lost my keys and my pet parakeet.
Bubbles rise with a joyful sound,
As I trip on the seaweed ground.

My goggles fog, I can't see clear,
A crab pinches my leg, oh dear!
Twisting through this underwater maze,
I ponder life in a salty haze.

A dolphin laughs, I'm quite a sight,
Flipping flippers in the pale moonlight.
"Grab a snack!" it seems to say,
While I float along in this fishy ballet.

When I resurface, what a surprise!
All the fish have won first place in prize.
I may be lost but I won't pout,
In the currents of humor, I'll wiggle about.

Captive in the Deep

Caught in a net of tangled hair,
A sea turtle offers me some hair.
We joke about our fashion sins,
While a sardine giggles, "You've got fins!"

Jellyfish float by, quite grand,
Dancing like they form a band.
With each sting, there's laughter and cheer,
"Don't go too close, my friend, I fear!"

I met a clam who plays the flute,
And sings of love, oh what a hoot!
Waves of humor crash all around,
In the depths, joy's easily found.

So let's embrace the quirks of this pit,
Though I'm "captive," I'm showing wit.
The ocean's a stage, let's play a part,
In this wild show, we'll steal each heart.

Odes to the Sunken Heart

In the wreckage of a sunken ship,
I found a sock, oh what a trip!
With mermaids singing their age-old tune,
I lost my shoes, but found a moon!

A pirate's ghost, with a cheeky grin,
Claims this is where the fun begins.
"Join my crew, don't be a sap,
We'll sail together, a treasure map!"

Octopuses juggling, what a sight,
They drop their balls in a flurry of plight.
"Don't mind us, we're just rehearsing,"
Their slippery squirts, my laughter's bursting!

So here's to hearts once filled with woe,
Dancing with the fish, putting on a show.
In this watery world, we play our part,
Laughter echoes in each sunken heart.

Silence of the Chambered Gloom

In a shell that whispers of days gone by,
I found a crab who fancied the sky.
"Why not hop!" he said with a grin,
"Let's escape this shell and join in!"

The deep-sea creatures gazed in delight,
As we traveled along, fish in sight.
We painted the reef with colors so bright,
In the gloom, our spirits took flight.

Anemones bloomed, swaying with grace,
We all broke the silence, a noisy embrace.
"Swim with their giggles," the sea spoke clear,
As laughter became the melody here.

So when gloom tries to pull us down,
We'll laugh in the dark, dance in our crown.
For even in depths that feel so profound,
A funny twist can always be found.

Chasing Lost Reflections

In a pond, a duck wears a hat,
Paddling along, how about that?
A fish waves back with a curious grin,
"Can you teach me your ways to swim?"

Bubbles rise, and I take a leap,
Of joy in the ripples, I barely keep.
The sun winks down, a playful tease,
Sprints of laughter float by on the breeze.

A turtle rolls over, quite proud of his shell,
"Join the races, it's fun, can't you tell?"
I trip on seaweed, but what do I care?
With giggles galore, I float without a care!

Mirrors of water, distorted and bright,
I see my reflection at least twice tonight!
Dancing with shadows, a comical show,
In the land of the lost, where all jokes flow.

Tides of the Unseen

Riding the waves on a giant whale's back,
He sings me a tune, I join in the pack.
A crab with a hat plays the saxophone,
"Come dance, my friend, in this underwater zone!"

The jellyfish twirl, a marvelous sight,
With glow-in-the-dark moves, they dazzle at night.
I try to keep up with their luminescent spree,
But instead, I get entangled, just look at me!

A seahorse giggles, I'm caught in his net,
Tangled in laughter, this night I won't forget.
He blows bubbles that pop with a cheerful sound,
Making friends at the depths, where few are found.

Mermaids compete in a splashy parade,
With glittery scales, they dance and they wade.
I join in their fun, though I may not fit,
A fish-out-of-water? No, just a quirky bit!

Beneath the Veil of Water

Under the surface, where secrets reside,
A penguin slips by on a joyride.
He wears cozy mittens, but how can he swim?
"It's chilly down here, but I'm never grim!"

An octopus chuckles, with eight arms in play,
Scribbling in currents where games come to stay.
He paints joyous colors on rocks all around,
With polka-dot fun, he turns frowns upside down!

The sun's just a twinkle, a distant delight,
As creatures collide in a whimsical fight.
I flip and I flounder, I tumble with glee,
In this playful ballet, oh, how wild it be!

Turtles giggle loud, trying to breakdance,
While minnows all whisper, "Give it a chance."
Under the veil, where laughter is free,
The heart of the ocean beats joyfully!

Lullabies from the Void

In the murky deep, the shadows do sway,
A crab tells a joke to pass on the way.
"Why didn't the fish go to school?" he snorts,
"Because it couldn't find its scales or sorts!"

An eel strums a tune on a seaweed guitar,
While starfish applaud from their rocky bazaar.
With giggles and wiggles, the night washes in,
While bubbles burst softly like a whimsical din.

I float on a wave, serenaded by cheers,
As clams share their tales built up over the years.
"We've lived through the tides, and not once did we pout!"
A clam cracks a grin as he whispers about.

In the twilight, where laughter mingles with dreams,
The ocean composes its sweet, funny themes.
As the night gently hums a lullaby's song,
I drift through the depths, where I truly belong.

Depths of the Unknown

In waters deep, I twirl and spin,
With flippers on, I think I'll win.
But down below, the fish all laugh,
I thought I'd float, but took a bath!

Bubbles rise with every kick,
A silly dance, a wobbly stick.
I wave to crabs, they wave me back,
And joke about my swimming knack!

I dive for pearls, but find old shoes,
Who knew the ocean had such views?
With treasure chests of socks and junk,
My prize finds make me feel so punk!

Seaweed wraps around my feet,
I shout, "Help!" but think it's sweet.
A playful wave, a splashy splash,
In the deep end, I make a splash!

Immersed in Shadows

In twilight depths, the shadows play,
They tickle toes in a sneaky way.
I'm grinning wide, but who can see,
The lurking fish are laughing at me!

I slip around like a slippery eel,
Attempting moves that make me squeal.
The jellyfish jiggle, they're quite the sight,
I dance with glee, but lose my flight!

A crab pinches me, what a cheeky prank,
I chase it off with a wobbly tank.
The rocks all snicker, the sea stars twirl,
I'm mighty brave, in this watery whirl!

With echoes of laughter, I take a dip,
The ocean's a ride, not a sinking ship.
So here I float, in giggles and glee,
Immersed in shadows, just fish and me!

Drowning in Echoes

Echos boing like rubber balls,
Through bubbles bright, they bounce off walls.
I shout, "Is it me?" but they just play,
The underwater joke, they snicker away!

With fins so bright, I swirl and spin,
But every turn, I'm met with chagrin.
The dolphins dance to my tune so wrong,
And play along in the craziest song!

Around the reef, I start to glide,
But fish all giggle, they won't let me hide.
With underwater monsters, I take my stand,
Just a clownish swimmer, feeling so grand!

Drowning in echoes, a comical plight,
I bob and weave, a hilarious sight,
The ocean's my stage, so come join the fun,
In this crazy game, we all can run!

Where Light Fades

Where light fades and shadows creep,
I flounder about, but can't find sleep.
My goggles fog, my vision's a mess,
Lost in the depths of this funny stress!

The octopus waves with a wiggly hand,
I wave back, but it's not quite planned.
"Help!" I call, "I'm stuck in a knot!"
They smirk and bubble, "You're quite the spot!"

With each splash and flip, I lose my way,
A tangled web where I love to play.
My thoughts are whirling, the silliness reigns,
In the twilight waters, there's humor in chains!

So here's to the fun where the light doesn't gleam,
A frolic in dark with a giggly dream.
With fishy friends and a buoyant heart,
We dive into laughter, that's just the start!

Shallows of the Forgotten

In waters where the sun forgot to gleam,
I met a fish with quite a silly dream.
He wore a hat that looked like a cheese,
And danced about with the utmost of ease.

The octopus winked with its many eyes,
Said, "Join my dance, don't be so shy!"
I slipped and tripped on the ocean floor,
Made a splash, they laughed, I wanted more.

Crabs clicked their claws in a beat so neat,
While jellyfish floated, swaying on their feet.
In the shallow waters, we played hide and seek,
Every squeal echoed, it was quite the peak.

But as I laughed and tumbled around,
A seahorse came by with a frown quite profound.
"You're making waves, you silly land brat!"
I grinned and replied, "Well, isn't that pat?"

The Deepening Abyss

In the depths where bubbles rise like dreams,
A whale was juggling a couple of beams.
"Try to catch this," he laughed with glee,
I leaped and missed, oh, woe is me!

The eels slithered by with a snaky dance,
"Join us!" they hissed, offering a chance.
But every twist made me more perplexed,
Tangled in laughter, oh, what a mess!

A clownfish cracked jokes, with colors so bright,
While the reef echoed with giggles at night.
"Why don't scientists trust the ocean?"
I shrugged and swayed, brimming with motion.

"Because it always has too many 'waves'!"
The sea creatures cheered for the laughs it gave.
And there I decided to dive even deeper,
Into this fun, where joy became a keeper.

The Silent Depths

In quiet moments where shadows blend,
A turtle spun tales about his best friend.
"A rock named Bob," he said with a grin,
"Was the greatest listener I ever did win!"

The seaweed giggled, swaying in sync,
While I tried to fathom, drowning in ink.
But as I pondered with great might,
A shrimp cracked jokes that felt just right.

"Why don't fish play piano?" he said with flair,
"Because you might get caught in the snare!"
The silence shattered, and laughter roared,
Among the depths where joy was stored.

And so we thrived in the silent spread,
With stories and spells until we were fed.
Enjoying life where shadows may creep,
In depths of laughter, we found our leap!

Shadows of the Ocean Floor

In shadows cast by the moonlit night,
A squid did a dance that was quite a sight.
He flipped and twirled with an elegant flair,
While sea stars cheered without a care.

"Have you heard the one about the stingray?"
A fish asked me, causing a swift sway.
"He wanted to fly and yell 'Look at me!'
But splashes just led him back to the sea!"

The octopus joined, his moves so slick,
"Two clams walk in, and one goes click!"
The laughter echoed around that dark place,
As shadows blended in a gentle embrace.

So down in the depths, we danced and we played,
Where worries dissolved like a sweet masquerade.
In shadows of laughter, we twirled till dawn,
For joy is forever where shadows are drawn.

Lost in the Blue

I dove in deep, thought I was cool,
Couldn't find my way, just a big ol' pool.
Fish swam past, they gave me a grin,
Said, "You lost, buddy? Where have you been?"

Tried to chat with a catfish named Lou,
He just stared back, said, "What's wrong with you?"
Thought I found treasure, just a shoe with a hole,
My underwater quest took quite the toll.

I made a friend, a crab on the prowl,
He pinched my toe and let out a howl.
Laughing so hard, I just couldn't stop,
In this vast ocean, I'm quite the flop!

Finally, I surfaced, took a big breath,
Yelled to the sky, "I've conquered my depth!"
But just then a wave splashed right in my face,
A fish swam by, giving me a race!

Silence of the Deep

In the silence of depths where the wobbly fish roam,
I tripped on a rock, made it quite my new home.
Starfish looked up, said, "You good, human?"
I waved back awkwardly, they smiled, in tune.

A turtle swam by, wearing a cool hat,
I asked him to share why he looked so fat.
He winked and he chuckled, said, "Just lots of greens,
Underwater dieting, no chips or machines."

I lost my way, got tangled in weeds,
Thought I found freedom, just mapped out the seeds.
Dolphins above were laughing and splashing,
While I wrestled a clam, our moves quite thrashing.

With laughter and waves, I made my return,
Promised the ocean, "Oh, I'll take my turn!"
But it pulled me back, with a whimsical breeze,
So I just danced along with jellyfish, wheeze!

Ghostly Waters

In spectral seas where the ghosts seem to wade,
I swam with the spirits, it sounds like a trade.
"Boo!" said a fish with a very round face,
I jumped and I laughed, found my own ghostly grace.

They floated around, in their sheets made of fins,
Turned out they were party-goers, full of grins.
A bubble popped loud, ghostly giggles abound,
Dancing with phantoms, oh, what a sound!

They taught me to ghost swim, to glide like a pro,
Through seaweed and coral, oh, my goodness, whoa!
Under the moon, in this watery bliss,
I took their advice and gave them a kiss.

But as dawn approached, they vanished so quick,
Leaving me wondering, "Was that just a trick?"
I chuckled to think, in this eerie green light,
The best of the fun happens just out of sight!

Submerged Dreams

In dreams where I floated, I soared with the breeze,
Worried I'd wake up and lose all my keys.
A jellyfish offered to hold them for me,
But said with a grin, "Only if you give tea!"

I bargained with bubbles, we struck up a deal,
A swim through the dreams of a dolphin's squeal.
We raced through the waters, it was quite the scene,
Colors and laughter, a vibrant routine.

I stumbled upon mermaids who longed for a dance,
Their glittery tails gave the waves quite a chance.
We twirled and we spun, swimming wild in the flow,
Till I snuck a whoopee cushion right under their glow!

With bubbles erupting, they laughed till they cried,
In my dreams of the deep, I felt like a guide.
Yet as I awoke, I smiled with glee,
For even in sleep, I can swim wild and free!

Surging with Shadows

In the depths where shadows play,
I met a fish who thought it could sway.
With a wink and a flip, it dashed near,
Said, "Come joyfully join my career!"

Chasing bubbles, I start to glide,
A jellyfish gives a wobbly ride.
Caught in the laughter, I twirl around,
What a goof, this underwater clown!

The eels are dancing, swaying in sync,
While the seaweed tickles, it makes me blink.
We're all just fish with a flair for the funny,
Why worry at depth when life's so sunny?

So splash and giggle, don't take a dive,
In this ocean, we feel so alive.
Let the shadows surge, let the laughter rise,
At the bottom of the sea, it's quite the surprise!

The Weight of the Depths

A crab in a top hat, oh what a sight,
Claiming to be the king of the night.
With a clatter of claws, he took his stance,
Said, "Join me for an underwater dance!"

A whale with a laugh, so grand and loud,
Swaying and swaying, oh, he's quite proud.
"I've got enough blubber for a laugh or two,
For the depths are heavy, but joy breaks through!"

Octopuses juggle, tossing shells high,
While sea stars giggle, a wink in their eye.
The weight of the depths is no cause for fear,
With friends all around, it's the best atmosphere!

Life down below, like a sitcom scene,
Comedy swims where it's never routine.
So when your heart sinks, just remember this,
In the weight of the depths, there's always bliss!

Call of the Watery Gloom

I heard a sound from the watery gloom,
A clam doing stand-up in a dark room.
With a scoff and a cough, he delivered a pun,
The octopus clapped, it was all in good fun!

A murky old squid with ink in the air,
Claimed he could paint, but was just full of flair.
He brushed his tentacles, swirled colors bright,
And we all chuckled till we lost the light.

A turtle in glasses, so wise and so slow,
Dished out advice with a wink and a glow.
"Life's like a wave; it comes and it goes,
Find humor in tides, and see how it flows!"

So heed the call from the gloomy deep,
Among the laughter, let your heart leap.
For even in darkness, fun's never shy,
In the watery gloom, it's a hilarious high!

The Abyss Stares Back

In the abyss, I found a cheeky shark,
He wore a bowtie and danced in the dark.
"Join me for tea, it's a lovely affair,
But watch for the piranhas, they love to snare!"

Bubbles float by as I'm sipping my brew,
A sense of oddity, yet nothing feels new.
"Life's but a jest, take a nibble or two,
The abyss stares back, but it giggles with you!"

Beneath every ripple, there's a story to share,
Like a starfish playing hopscotch without care.
"Don't fear the dark, it's a quirky old friend,
With a twist and a turn, joy and laughter blend!"

So dance in the depths, let your spirit unstack,
For laughter is endless, no matter the whack.
In the tides of the strange, you'll find what you lack,
When the abyss stares, laugh loud and come back!

Shrouded in Liquid Night

Flippers flail like seagulls' wings,
In waters dark, the laughter sings.
Rubber ducks bob, quacking a tune,
While mermaids giggle 'neath the moon.

Goggles fog up like a mystery clue,
I glide through dreams where I can't turn blue.
A splash, a swirl, oh what a sight!
Chasing fish in a dance of delight.

Bubbles rise with each silly joke,
Tickling toes, oh what a poke!
The deep is here, but I am bold,
With every stroke, more stories told.

My buoyant waist, it tells no lie,
A floating noodle, oh me, oh my!
In this liquid realm, I am the star,
Just don't forget where you left your car.

Haunting Depths of Solitude

Down in the depths where fish do swim,
I ponder life on a whim.
Octopus tickles my silly nose,
While sardines dance in their cute little rows.

Lonely seaweed waves hello,
Swaying gently in the undertow.
Crustaceans chatting with my toes,
They tell the best jokes, goodness knows!

Echoes of laughter fill my ear,
As I pretend to steer a grand mirror.
Bubble-blowing with great finesse,
Each plop and pop—a true messy success.

But wait! A shark with a goofy grin,
"Wanna race?" Oh let the fun begin!
I splash and dash, the sea my stage,
In this solitude, I'm free to engage.

The Moan of Drowned Dreams

Bubbles whisper secrets of days gone by,
I float like pizza on a cheese-filled sky.
Drowned dreams bob like corks, you see,
Pretending they're a part of me.

A fish with glasses gives me a wink,
"Join the party, come have a drink!"
We sink and rise in our silly game,
Practicing strokes that all sound the same.

Seashells gossip in a churning swirl,
Whispering tales as the currents twirl.
My dreams may sink, but laughter lifts,
In this abyss, come find the gifts!

Tangled nets of forgotten schemes,
All drifting off like fading dreams.
In the depths, I'll find some fun,
With each goofy flip, a new life begun.

Sinking with Grace

I dive into depths with my goofy flair,
Flipping and floundering without a care.
My swimsuit squeaks with every move,
Making waves in this quirky groove.

Down, down I go, like a graceful frog,
Wiggling through kelp like a silly log.
Fins for flying, but I'm stuck in the muck,
Laughing at how I've lost all my luck.

In this blue soup, I spin and whirl,
Bubbles popping like a wild twirl.
Mermaids applaud from their watery throne,
While sea cucumbers call me their own.

Yet somehow, I take this ridiculous fall,
Every splashy sink is a giggly call.
So here I float, in style and grace,
Finding joy in this watery place.